Speak and Spell

POEMS BY
ALLISON JOSEPH

GLASS LYRE PRESS

Copyright © 2022 Allison Joseph
Paperback ISBN: 978-1-941783-87-0

All rights reserved: Except for the purpose of quoting brief passages for review, no part of this book may be reproduced or transmitted in any form or by any means, electronic or mechanical, including photocopying, recording, or by any information storage and retrieval system, without permission in writing from the publisher.

Design & Layout: Steven Asmussen
Cover Photo: Allison Joseph

Glass Lyre Press, LLC
P.O. Box 2693
Glenview, IL 60025
www.GlassLyrePress.com

Speak and Spell

CONTENTS

Speak	1
If Purses Had Mouths	2
Dressing Down	3
August Morning, in the Mirror	5
Minor Ailments	6
Household Duties	9
Could You Ask Somebody Else (I'm Already Committed)	11
Black	12
Sloth	13
Traveling Alone	14
Entreaty	15
Seduction in Blues	16
Procession	17
Visiting Hours	18
Compensation	19
In Caves with Poets	20
A Triolet for Crapsey	21
Spell for Welcoming a Poem into the World	22
About the Author	23

Speak

Resolve for me the poem of your life,
let loose the worlds your words contain.
Allow the life you've lived to come to air.

Give voice to all encounters of the skin—
let loose the worlds your words contain.

Explain to me the logic of your thought;
the way you view the world is puzzling, strange.
Explain to me where each new scar is from.

Discuss with me your doubt of solid things–
the way you view the world is puzzling, strange,

and hard to comprehend. I want to know
how surfaces appear to you, what gives
you fevered dreams and phantom pains.

You say you can't describe
how surfaces appear to you. What gives

you fevered dreams and phantom pains?
Explain to me where each new scar is from.
Resolve for me the poem of your life.

If Purses Had Mouths

If purses had mouths, mine would shout,
*stop stuffing me with all this crap—broken
pencils, rolls of undeveloped film you took
years ago, receipts from Best Buy and
T.J. Maxx*, where you've bought
way too much and not enough.
If purses had mouths, mine would whine
*don't spend any more money on chocolate
because only greedy you gets to taste
that sweetness, while I only get wrappers.*
If purses had mouths, mine would nag,
*you idiot, don't you remember you put
your keys in my inside zipper pocket.
Stop running around your messy house
cursing and crying that you can't find
them, when all you have to do is look
inside my lining.* If purses had mouths,
mine would be pissed at the way
I sling her on the floor, toss her under
the bed, leave her to die of heatstroke
in the car. If purses had mouths,
mine would sputter: *so long, goodbye,
sayonara, get another lackey to tote
all your unimportant memos, letters,
your money and chewing gum, your
nasty tissues. Get a life,* my purse
says, its brown leather cracking, its
zipper too tired to close itself up.

Dressing Down

How free it is to be homely,
to walk streets unfettered
by the lavish complications
of ornate jangles of jewelry,

taut skirts, restrictive belts,
and high heels, my broad frame
no longer teetering shaky
above sidewalks. I know

my face is plain, undistinguished
by trend or fashion: mascara
absent from my lashes,
eye shadow not lurking

in the creases of my lids,
no harsh brow pencil lines
drawn to groom the unruly
thickets above my eyes,

eyes I don't care to alter
with contact lenses' false hues.
What pleasure there is
in shoes broken down

at their heels, what gladness
in avoiding the tyranny of pantyhose
binding my belly, holding me
in so tight I can't walk, can't run,

can't move. In my shabby coat,
I'm a happy tramp, unperturbed
by sudden accidents of wind,
sweat, or weather—no make-up

to smudge, no dress to rip,
nothing but this homely face
to present to the world—
this nose not narrowed,

these cheeks not rouged,
these lips delicate in their
lack of manufactured color—
pink, pliant, perfectly poised.

August Morning, in the Mirror

I can't decide which face to wear today:
the surly look nobody's eyes will meet,
the scowl that twists my lips, the frown.
Why act as if I really want to greet
the foes and friends I'd rather shoo away,
and keep them from my business, keep life neat?
Why act as if I really want to greet
my mirthless face— my sleepy eyes cast down,
my motions slowed by steamy summer heat?
I can't decide which face to wear today.

Minor Ailments

My eye won't stop twitching;
it's more nervous than I am,

announcing its anxieties
to anyone who looks closely.

And anyone who looks closely
will also see the blemishes

that rise in ridges across
my cheeks, imperfections

no amount of scrubbing
can remedy. My hair's

not right, drier
than before, as if

my shampoo quit working,
or some vitamin's in

short supply, making me
bleaker, wearier, less able.

But who wants to bother
the medical profession

with complaints too common
to be interesting, maladies

so bland they don't merit
an aspirin's worth of attention.

Amazing how the body can go astray
in all sorts of minute ways:

deviations of breath, lungs
less capable, deviations

of flesh, legs less capable,
deviations of the heart,

its beat thudding my chest
as if it no longer wants

to be there, craving space
in a younger, stronger body.

These little aches, niggling
cramps, these anxiety lines

creeping around my eyes—
I'd be lying if I said

they didn't bother me,
lying if I told you I wasn't

taken aback by the first gray strand
I found in my husband's lush hair.

But because it was his, from him
and of him, I loved that little

sign of aging, that pale affliction,
knew I could learn to live

with my own tiny ills—
the split seconds lost

from my timing, the wheeze
in my chest from inhaling

too-cold winter winds,
the creak in my bones

on too-cold winter nights.
This isn't suffering, not

legitimately so, it's only breath
and body running out—of time, of life.

Household Duties

Don't think I'll ever find joy
in these unchanging, unending tasks,
that I'll ever find satisfaction

in clean, scrubbed, shining sinks
empty of plates, saucers, utensils,
countertops unsoiled by crumbs

or spills, desktops free of
mug stains, coffee rings,
sticky spots gone

from my single-ply carpet.
Unlike the smiling women
regularly sighted on television,

my life isn't consumed
by relentless searches
for detergent that leaves clothes

smelling fresher, looking brighter,
boosters that will get my laundry
whiter than I ever thought

it could be, cleansers that leave
my bathtub spotless, not scratching
its finish. Will someone tell me why

cleanliness is next to Godliness,
as if cleanliness should be next
to anything at all, chemists working

in labs the world over
to concoct even fiercer cleaners
for my bathroom, kitchen,

the scary nook behind my
refrigerator, cozy niche
for dust bunnies, spiderwebs.

The television pitchwomen
grin about how much better
their lives have become —

thanks to the newest brand
of liquid deodorizing cleanser,
the newest spray bottle

of glorious, victorious bleach,
crazy about the latest
most marvelous dishwasher powder,

now with thirty-five percent more
fighting power. It makes them
thirty-five percent happier,

thirty-five percent more secure
that someone like me
won't come to their spotless homes,

tracking dirt all over
the no-wax floors they've just
given the polishing of a lifetime.

Could You Ask Somebody Else (I'm Already Committed)

I promise too many people
too many things, scribble
to-do lists on the backs
of torn envelopes I then

cannot locate, scrawl addresses
and directions on snatches of paper
I lose within my purse's depths,
book bag's recesses. Grocery

lists, appointment cards,
time-sensitive memos, overdue
bills, overstuffed envelopes
of unanswered correspondence

all scatter all over my desk,
deepening the channel of guilt
burrowing through my stomach's
lining, corrosive trail I assuage

with swigs from that bottle
of pink candy-colored liquid
also on my desk. I greet everyone
with my *hi-sorry-I should-have*

had-that-for-you yesterday smile,
my *yes-I'll-have-it-for-you-soon*
stammer. And I slink away,
already starting to forget

what I'd promised to remember,
already forgetting what I'd signed.
Remind me again
what I said I'd do for you?

Black

after the quilt by JoAnna Johnson

This quilt says mourning gown
for a girl who didn't live to see
twelve, drab garb now pinned

to the gallery's walls, a dress
the color of a garbage bag with its
Peter Pan collar, its three-quarter

sleeves long enough to cover some
scars, not all. Locked inside her coffin,
did she wear a dress like this one,

her mourners also in black, sober
men and women now weary
after the long search's end—

all sifting of rocks, roots, trees, and
riverbanks done, the barking dogs
that found her still perking alert ears?

Step closer and orange stitches appear,
wind through black cloth in contours
of roses, eyes, circles, roads that twist

through underbrush where anyone
could fall, or be hidden. Closer still
and black becomes gray, and that gray

shimmers, light within gloom,
color of an overcast sky gone to storm.
Touch it. It's not like cloth at all, no give.

No girl could wear this, except in death.

Sloth

Call it luxury instead: life steeped in inactivity,
a lovely languor too good to shake, a technique

easily honed on any sofa, couch, or bed.
Simply stretch out fully, let limbs loosen

and go slack, tension ebbing out of your body
through the fingertips, toes. Have someone

bring you pillows for head and foot, soft
mounds to rely on as you drift in and out

of sleep, conscious of only your own
light breathing. Settle into the pleasure

of doing nothing, enjoy hours when nothing
occupies you but your own off-key singing,

a bit of absent-minded music. You're a creature
of no speed, no movement or action, no purpose

but being in the world, refraining
from the mind's work. You're curled

away where no one can touch you,
indolence so complete no one dares

come within five feet of you, afraid to ruin
the most tranquil laziness in the world.

Traveling Alone

for JT

I always miss you most
when coming back to you
from some faraway coast,
some unfamiliar view.

The closer I arrive,
the further that I feel.
Airports are netherworlds
where nothing is revealed.

I want to glimpse your face
before I know I can,
impatient for the place
where I'll see you again—

no crowded airplane aisles,
no evening flight delays.
I want to shrink the miles
until they fall away—

no suitcases to claim,
no rush hour to fight.
I'd like to blink my eyes,
come home without a flight.

At home at last with you
and weary from my life,
I'm private once again,
unfettered as your wife.

Entreaty

Better wear your raincoat,
better wear your shoes.
Bitter drizzle's coming,
weather for the blues.

Darkness soon will cover
all that you can see,
better listen, brother,
wait to hear from me.

Winter settles sudden,
moaning weary winds.
No one's stirring, moving,
no messages from friends.

Windows creaking open,
shutters clang and bash.
Sodden broken branches—
hear them thud and crash.

Let me warm your body,
let me keep you well.
Let me be the woman
to break this season's spell.

Seduction in Blues

Have you seen how my eyes shine,
how they glow a glossy brown?
Have you seen how my eyes shine,
yes, they glow a glossy brown.
If you only look you'll notice
just what you have around.

You haven't tasted my lips yet,
nor felt my rumbling hips?
No, you haven't tasted my lips yet,
nor felt my rumbling hips.
You should feel just how I flow—
better than liquor, quicker than whips.

But you keep trying to escape—
you say I hold you down.
Yes, you keep trying to escape—
you swear I hold you down.
But my door swings wide and open,
my mouth not fixed in frown.

So I invite you—stay at home,
seek here the stroke you're after.
So I entice you—stay at home,
stroke here just what you're after.
My bed is meant for motion—
my bed resounds in laughter.

Procession

You turn your face away from mine
so I can't see the tears you wipe
from off your cheeks. It's not a sign
of grief you share; you're not that type.

You turn your face away
though I know I should
find something apt to say,
I wish I only could.

You turn your face,
then wipe each cheek;
I can't erase
this awkward week.

You turn
to join the line
of loss, your features stern.
You turn your face away from mine.

Visiting Hours

I know the dreary walls of hospitals,
the convoluted corridors and wards
where pain comes audibly in sighs
and whispers, screams and coughs.
I come at the appointed hours,

aware that these aren't simply hours—
afraid to glimpse emaciated men
shuffle nowhere with their IVs, coughs
rattling their fractured bodies, afraid to hear
mothers of terminal children sigh,

faces careworn. Another wheeze, cough,
another gray-faced child with a shaved scalp.
I find I'm holding in my sighs—
it's my own mother who's terminal,
her body in a bed deep within these wards

where machines snap on with a whoosh, a sigh,
metallic equipment keeping her lungs alive, clear,
so I can dread these walls, these wards
one more time, one more stint of hours,
one more walk from car to hospital.

Compensation

There are so few rewards for writing verse—
no luxuries for making words behave.
Is poetry a blessing or a curse?

As a career, there's nothing worse
than making poems no one craves.
There are so few rewards for writing verse.

Some other job will fatten up your purse
and bring you fame, or make you brave.
Is poetry a blessing or a curse?

Try management or be a nurse—
or be a priest, serene and grave.
There are so few rewards for writing verse.

So, poetry? It's like a hearse,
a memory no one wants to save.
Is poetry a blessing or a curse?

This act of words won't reimburse
your love; it's writers who end up depraved.
There are so few rewards for writing verse—
is poetry a blessing or a curse?

In Caves With Poets

Blanchard Springs Caverns, Arkansas

All week long we haven't been able to shut up,
so it took something this grand to stop our speech,
make us *ooh* and *aah* because words aren't enough.

We've paid six dollars each to descend
by elevator into this cold sculpted earth,
man-made concrete steps helping us through

formations of slick rock, staggered cliffs.
We shiver from the chill, our tour guide
chiding us not to fall behind, footing slippery

though aided by an iron railing along steps
that descend and descend, winding
and twisting down into these crevices of earth,

stalactites and stalagmites glowing
in the stutter of flashlights. Outside
Arkansas summer sweats, but down here

we wiggle life back into clammy fingers,
snap photos that can't capture how this earth
yielded to water, how water caused this drama.

A Triolet for Crapsey

Some lives are tragic and obscure—
a poet lives, then dies, alone,
like Adelaide before the cure.
Some lives are tragic and obscure—
no matter how her words might lure,
she's trivia, a great unknown.
Some lives are tragic and obscure.
A poet lives, then dies, alone.

Spell For Welcoming a Poem Into the World

Lighten your limbs in the rhythm of words
    you have never paired before, words
        anxious as midnight wails,
            soothing as red velvet cake.
Let your body, that sapling, sway
    like slimmest switches cut from a tree
        too young to be scarred by fire.
Whether sitting or standing, move
    from side to side, your body
        a wave, a spill, a drum
            only you can sound.
Let palms discover blank page newness,
    see letters take shape on the page
        before you write them down:
    O's as round as eyes, l's looping crazily
    as a listing rollercoaster.
Let language control your diligent hands—
    this time not the time for dishwashing
        or pot-scrubbing—give this page
            all it wants, all you can manage.
Then, when you are done, bundle your poem
    carefully, gather pages one by one
        so you can whisper these new words
        into the best available ear,
your listener's face transformed on hearing
    words you never knew could come from you.

About the Author

Allison Joseph currently lives, teaches, and writes in Carbondale, Illinois, where she is part of the creative writing faculty at Southern Illinois University. Her most recent collections of poems are *Any Proper Weave* (Kelsay Books, 2022), *Lexicon* (Red Hen Press, 2021), *Professional Happiness* (Backbone Press, 2021), and *Confessions of a Barefaced Woman* (Red Hen Press, 2018). *Confessions of a Barefaced Woman* won the 2019 Feathered Quill Book Award and was a finalist in the poetry category for the 2019 NAACP Image Award. Her poems have appeared in the *New York Times* and in the Best American Poetry Series. She is the widow of poet and editor Jon Tribble.

Glass Lyre Press

exceptional works to replenish the spirit

Glass Lyre Press is an independent literary publisher interested in technically accomplished, stylistically distinct, and original work. Glass Lyre seeks diverse writers that possess a dynamic aesthetic and an ability to emotionally and intellectually engage a wide audience of readers.

Glass Lyre's vision is to connect the world through language and art. We hope to expand the scope of poetry and short fiction for the general reader through exceptionally well-written books, which evoke emotion, provide insight, and resonate with the human spirit.

Poetry Collections
Poetry Chapbooks
Select Short & Flash Fiction
Anthologies

www.GlassLyrePress.com

www.ingramcontent.com/pod-product-compliance
Lightning Source LLC
Chambersburg PA
CBHW030142100526
44592CB00011B/1015